SCARSDALE

Dan O'Brien, author of *War Reporter* (CBe, 2013; winner of the Fenton Aldeburgh Prize for a first collection of poetry), is a playwright and poet living in Los Angeles. He was born in Scarsdale, New York, in 1973. His play *The Body of an American* won the Horton Foote Prize and the inaugural Edward M. Kennedy Prize for Drama, and had its European premiere in London in 2014.

'Dan O'Brien is one of our keenest observers of domestic life. From the grass growing greener next door to the wildlife that haunts vacation spots, even down to the knot in a boy's tie, this book is generously affectionate yet sharply alert to both the details and dramas in family life. Not for nothing can the word "scar" be found in the name "Scarsdale", but as this fine poet shows, we can bear the past bravely, and come away from it, as we do from his book, deeply enriched.'
– Don Share

From reviews of *War Reporter*:

'A masterpiece of truthfulness and feeling, and a completely *sui generis* addition not just to writing about war but to contemporary poetry' – Patrick McGuinness, *Guardian*

'*War Reporter* is visceral, disturbing, at times consoling, and always honest. O'Brien's work is an incredible achievement. Anyone who cares about how we go to war – and how we return – must read it.' – *Slate*

'I commend this work for its great originality, courage and humanity.' – Fergal Keane

also by Dan O'Brien

War Reporter

Dan O'Brien

SCARSDALE

ACKNOWLEDGEMENTS *2River View* ('The Firecracker', 'The Worm'); *32 Poems* ('The Dead End', 'Hardwick, VT', 'Patience'); *Alaska Quarterly Review* ('My Handwriting'); *America* ('God's Brother'); *Apple Valley Review* ('Mormons'); *Bare Fiction* ('The Bat', 'Four Signs', 'A Leaf', 'Truro', 'A Visit'); *Cold Mountain Review* ('Fixing the House', 'The House in Scarsdale'); *Crab Orchard Review* ('A Box of Oranges'); *Ellipsis* ('Where You From?'); *Georgetown Review* ('Breaking the Ice'); *Greensboro Review* ('Danvers Wedding', 'Meat on the Fire'); *Hampden-Sydney Poetry Review* ('Bluefish', 'The Wooden Box'); *Iodine* ('First Pages of a New Journal', 'Via Waterford'); *Iron Horse Literary Review* ('Gone Dog', 'Pearl River'); *Lilliput Review* ('My Mother'); *Linebreak* ('Scrupulosity'); *Louisville Review* ('Greenwich / Isle of Dogs'); *Margie* ('Five-and-Dime, Scarsdale'); *The Midwest Quarterly* ('Raccoons'); *New South* ('Bread Loaf 1994'); *Nimrod* ('Another Complaint'); *The Owls* ('From Larchmont'); *Red Lion Square* ('Mice'); *The South Carolina Review* ('Blue Nun', 'Pay Phone'); *Southern Humanities Review* ('The Knot'); *storySouth* ('The Music House'); *Tuesday; An Art Project* ('Black Pool'); *UCity Review* ('After the Service', 'The Amphitheatre', 'Castle White Apartments')

First published in 2014
by CB editions
146 Percy Road London W12 9QL
www.cbeditions.com

Printed in England by Blissetts, London W3 8DH

ISBN 978-1-909585-02-7

For my brother

Come back, come back . . . my wretched, feeble and unwanted child.

– John Cheever

Contents

My Handwriting

grew small for a time, Puritan
in the black ink I still favor. I felt compelled
to rein myself in, believing
the sin of pride governed me,
a child. I thought large print meant loud voice
and loud voice an affront
to God's ears. So I chastened myself to grow smaller
while still remaining
the great thing I was, still decipherable
to myself at least,
and if not to me then to God.

I had other sins, of course,
and prayers I knew by heart.

Or did I dwindle myself down
to this thread on the page
so my mother would find me
and ask, What's this?

Breaking the Ice

Snow fell, stopped
as evening fell; Father said,
Clear the walk. I did. Down deep the snow
was ice. One can only get the stones
so clean; and these slates out back
were riotous, decayed.

I came inside to eat.
He sent me out again, no dinner,
put a hoe in my hands. Break it up, he said,
then shovel it all away. I did.

That gold cube of light
in the kitchen overhead
with my family inside speaking: I believed
this gift will save me
in time.

God's Brother

We walked home
from school; he was
older than I was
by ages. The hill
was a runnel of shade
as the great trees discarded
their leprous bark down
to the pavement, curling
and trod into dust. I told him
of a boy who'd misbehaved
at school, again. What makes you
think you're better
than him? he asked.

We walked in silence after that, wet leaves
under our feet
like water.

Then as if to remind us both
he said, You're not God,
you know.

The Bat

She was terrified
of the bat as it beat on
the walls and ceiling of
our room on the ground
floor of that motel
in sunlight in morning.

If a bird is trapped
inside
an angel is here. What then is
the bat?

Its insane
fur and black skin clapping
while I rolled an orange
back and forth
on the bedspread.

Why were we here?
For some reason,
surely. But was it
sunny, in the story?
She'd say for years she fought the bat
with a broom.
And where was my father
in all this?

Just me and my despairing mother,
the bat, the orange, the broom,

and finally a man
who came and caught
the bat in his hands, and gently
gave it back to the trees.

Who was our hero?
Was he also me?

Scrupulosity

Our father and I are down on our knees
with razor blades in our hands
and rags in a bucket to wipe away
the glue. This ancient glue is like the blood
in the heart of a lamb we dissected
in school. Making black crescents of our nails,
staining the heels of our hands, turpentine
won't bring it up alone. So we scrape
the scabrous floor raw with our blades until
our wrists and fingers ache. We do not speak
a word, only breathing hard and dripping sweat
into the clots we brush away. Listening
to the grind of the blade and the slap
of the rag, the hitch in Father's throat,
his low, anxious breaking of wind. Like monks,
he says. Or do I imagine he's spoken
to me? His father died young,
of his heart. His face flushes, the vein
in his forehead arises. He tells me
to finish on my own. I'm glad when he's gone,
I breathe easier. I work harder
now too, on my knees, this monk
whose fingers ache for God. When he returns
he'll find our floor is finished, perfect soon.

The Dead End

We hated in silence
the family that lived
between us and the swamp,
as we called this
vacant lot of brush, all tangled
with skeins of wild grapes, skunk
cabbage and moss that soaked
through our thin soles. They told us
to stay out; but every day
we disobeyed, beating
our sticks into swords, burning
garbage and breathing in
such dismal fumes. Humping
each other's blue jeans
on discarded cushions
damp with rain. A brook

seeped through a culvert clogged
with rotting leaves, broken
bottle glass and rusted
batteries. In winter
this mud sludge froze over.
When we'd fall through we'd pull
ourselves free, the feathers
in our down coats clinging
like shame. Our bald father
would decry the local
municipality: If only
they'd dredge the old brook – then
it would flow clean and clear
to the ocean
like it used to in the days before
you six were born.

Raccoons

Rarely we heard them, only
some nights the lupine mewling
of their fighting or fucking
beneath our windows. Rarely
we saw them either, unless
we were waiting; and then
here they'd come, a family
with eyes like a line of fireflies
in one rapacious, humpbacked
drive. Because every evening

they'd return with their dexterous,
almost human hands, and leave the grass
littered with our shame: diapers
full of shit, carcasses
of chicken roasters, tampons, our father's
condoms – all strung out
in the pachysandras, all caught
in the teeth of a rotting
backyard fence. All cooking in the sun
and the heavenly rattle
of the August cicadas. Desecrated further
by their scat like berries flung
and popping with flies. He dropped

firecrackers from the kitchen
window, into the yawn of
the open trash cans. And we laughed
as they tumbled out, staggering
in the grass, shaking the din
from their animal brains. They climbed
back in again, always. – How dumb!
we'd say. – What thugs! One night he shot two

raccoons while we were sleeping
but the next morning saw
they were still breathing,
paralyzed. He was afraid
our neighbors would hear gunshots
before breakfast, so taking
our baseball bat he smashed
their skulls in. Our mother
found this humorous somehow,
a testament to our father's
secret value. We buried them

discreetly in the roots
of an azalea bush. The dirt
was soft where we filled that hole
for years. I would ask
myself, Can animals haunt . . . ?
You must never tell a soul
what happened out there, he told
Mother, and Mother
told us.

Mice

Upstate with water
too cold for swimming
in a lake of mud
and stone, lapped by waves
of mysterious
origin: a man seized
and lifted me up
in his arms
for running around
the porch that encircled
his mostly empty
inn. That night she saw

a mouse in the rooms
of the house we shared
with a family
we never saw; who came and went
by a different door,
but at night we'd hear
their boisterous voices
ascending the stairs
on the other side
of the wall. I hear
the mice in the walls,
she said. So we stalked

that sound, kept vigil
in chairs by the fire
with rackets and bats
and brooms, listening
for the scrape and the scratch
and the squeal. Drifting off
to sleep, failing
her again, dreaming

of the scraping step,
the squealing laughter
ascending the stairs.

Blue Nun

How sophisticated, brave
we thought they both were to drink
Blue Nun. While my mother cooked
joylessly, and the old man
watched the news. Considering
her mother would beat her when blind drunk,
and his mother had been trying
to join his father in death
for years, once stepping out of bed
into a shattered ankle, drunk. You must stay
away, they'd warn us. They stayed away,
too. Except for those rare evenings
when for mysterious reasons
she'd park outside the pricey
wine store downtown, to purchase
her bottle of Blue Nun – what I like
to imagine they first tasted
in somebody's basement
in high school, or the evening
of their so-called elopement
upstate somewhere. She'd sip
over the bubbling gray ground meat
in the crowded pan. Her eyes wet
with some kind of inward, chastised
release. And sometimes he'd bring his
next glass to the table
and tell such funny stories!
that she'd watch him with both fear
and pleasure: here was a man
she hardly knew.

A Box of Oranges

Each year the box came early, a month before Christmas
at least, and stayed there for ages, sometimes a week
in shadow in the mornings, and then sunlight as the day
spread across our kitchen floor. We all knew what was inside:
oranges we'd never eat, and a note signed from someone
we'd never met, but of whom we'd hear the occasional,
apocryphal gripe, whenever our mother was feeling forlorn
or besieged (which was all the time really): how she'd beat
our mother; how she'd had a son go insane, get sent away
to Canada, somewhere. Her husband never came home.
She was beautiful, a blonde, and she'd take a daughter
out of school with her to go see movies in the daytime . . .

These oranges would be bruised, shrunken, mottled with mold,
wrapped up in a pink girlish gauze. As a chore we'd discover
each lumped globe, then set them upon our gloomy sideboard
gently, as if a voice constrained within might somehow speak
       to us . . .

Years later we met her in the garden of our aunt's house
sitting in a folding lawn chair; imperiously she held her cheek
       up
to the sun. Her back turned to her four estranged, estranging
daughters: she was my mother – exactly like my mother
is today. I don't remember her speaking a word all that
       afternoon . . .

After the Service

After the service was over
and the children had all gone home,
as the parkway roared
like a Pentecost, and the sky
was a hazy premonition
of every profound
hurt to come – how strong
I felt! What a lesson
I was learning. No one needs anyone,
really. Tossing loose cement
against a crumbling cement wall
in the parking lot of the church, as the crows
bounced into the branches; waiting
for you to come and take me home,
whenever that hour should come.

Hardwick, VT

One's own mother desired
by strangers:
                on a lakeshore
of imported sand, where
two local types watched
from their pickup atop
the berthing ramp, rifles
in the gun rack behind
their covered heads. Drinking
beers from cans. They watched her
moving in her bathing suit
with a sullen pride
like hate. All that summer

I couldn't stop dribbling
my soccer ball around
our rented house. We had found
our doctor's pills
in the couch. Our brother
who'd tried to kill himself
was home, alone. The woods
were dark and deep. The phone

would sometimes ring at night,
but there would never be
anyone there, only
breath or the sound
of static. All that summer
we held our breaths whenever
a pickup rolled down
our road that went nowhere.

The Knot

The occasional morning
I was required to dress
like a man and not this
boy I was, Mother would send me
upstairs to you, to tie
the knot of my tie. This tie
was yours anyway. I'd ask
if I might wear it again,
having kept it with me since
the last time; amazed always
when you said, All right. Upright
in front of you and Mother's
twin mirrors in the watery
winter light, while your fingers
worked the silken length,
then reworking, folding
the tie over, then around,
over and up to
my thin throat; having to start over
when the length turned out all wrong,
before turning brusquely down
the collar with your whistling
breath, your small eyes tightening on
the knot. I'm always surprised
you never taught me how
to do this for myself. I'm not surprised
I never learned.

Pearl River

One of the rare stories
he'd tell. Of drifting downriver at dawn
with friends. Not fishing
but shooting the water
rats on the farthest shore,
underneath the rotting
-down wharves. He said he would know
his prey by the flickering
fire of the rising
sun in their eyes. This tale

he'd tell with such flashing
joy in his eyes! So proud
to prove something. That rifle
he'd oil in the bedroom
each spring. Our mother he'd nail
each Sunday morning
to their bed. Yet never any sense

of music in the man, so the meaning
of his stories remains
almost entirely obscure.

The Worm

Alone in the boat
with you, rowing out
on the lake. Take
the Styrofoam cup
and with my fingers
dig through the fecal
loam. For night crawlers,
blood suckers. His cold
striated, mucoid
skin, pink bulbous band
like a prepuce. You
show me how to hold
the naked, the tangling
thread, then push the barbed
hook through. Once, then twice
till the bait's a balled
crucifix of dirt. Don't
be a faggot,
you say as you cast
your line out. I drop
the live worm between
my bare knees, puncture
its middle, watch its
hermaphroditic
tail flipping blind. Ooze
spotting the wood grain
green. Then casting out
the loose loop, I see
my poor worm sinking
beneath the rhythmic
lozenges of light. Such grace
when the hook comes back
clean. One time I left

the worms on their hooks
and smiled when I saw
you searching the house
for the source of all
that smell of death.

Bluefish

I

Our sister cries when she must stand
beside our cousin girls. They're gay
and pretty as she knows she'll never be.
Our brothers are pitied by us all.
Boy cousins, there are three,
a near-symmetry that seems to mock
our poverty. They mock us
playfully. They're athletes
who drink beer and break windows
with errant lacrosse balls, while we read books
and must remain inherently
uncouth. I aspired to be like them
one day, to keep my father's pride
in mind while living my life out
in the fields. I'd throw the ball
and save the glass and show them all I
was the fruit of their blood's design.

In truth, one was an alcoholic,
one a poet who never wrote.
One wrecked cars every chance he got.
One starved herself, while another
got beaten by her boyfriend.
Their mother ate, their father fished
Long Island Sound: gray miracle of bluefish
pulled living from the deep.

2

Gray miracle of bluefish pulled living
from the deep: my uncle married my mother's sister
and made a Catholic out of her, sold dress shirts her father made
in Bangalore, wore sandals he called Jesus-shoes
to walk upon the waves, should his bark break apart
and sink beneath the Sound.

                                        My uncle took us out at dawn; I got sick,
disgraced: the sun was too strong. I was too delicate,
I feared. Sitting in shade and watching what they caught,
I felt more fear than pity
when they dropped them in the pail to drown
on air.

          Until a confusion of currents and wakes
shook our sides and spilt all that glitter of the dying blue-fish
like coins
– they flexed their scales and gasped their blood-caked gills
until my uncle beat them with a stick
kept for that purpose and
their blood streaked the scum-slick deck.

                                        In dock,

tied up, he sliced out their spines
and scooped out their guts
and dropped it all down
onto his sandaled toes. But a blackfish
had been caught:
mean, thorny and strange. My uncle held him
to gut him – he leapt and the knife
sliced into my uncle's hand
as the blackfish
slipped back into
the Sound.

Mormons

Their lawn was so much greener than ours, thanks to all
their weekend ministrations, down on their knees
behind the thorn hedge, he in his short sleeves and dungarees
and John Deere cap; she in her jogging suit
always, smiling sweetly with the elderly
poodle of the Hebraic name languishing
on a chain beside her in the grass. They'd give us tomatoes
at the end of summer, robust, ripe, suspiciously red.
We'd set them on the windowsill. Afraid
to eat them, naturally. What made their garden grow
so well was all the chemicals they'd use.
Only some Mormons from Nevada . . . our father
liked to say, shaking his head with disbelief
at the trust of such a people! as if they believed
they'd never die, they were loved by God so well.

These were the only people our father could admire,
so we almost became like them. Every Sunday
we'd entertain two young blond missionaries
in their funereal suits; we kept their Book
of Mormon on my mother's bedside table,
as our basement filled up with buckets
of dried milk, honey, rice and distilled water,
enough to keep us alive long after that nuclear fire
God promised for next time. But something stopped us

from converting. The young blond missionaries
stopped coming, and our Book of Mormon disappeared
inside my mother's bedside table, beneath
her diaphragm, her self-help books, her unused
diaries. All that food we ate up by degrees
without joy or irony. Our mother would say
she'd been the one to disagree with their law

that all wives must go to hell – or wherever
their husbands are sent. It's not fair, she'd tell us,
to punish a woman for her husband's sins.

The Bear

I hate to be the bear
of bad tidings, the stranger at the door
seemed to say. I listened
behind my father's back. Then raced upstairs
to tell them all
the news. All that next day we waited,

tossing pebbles
into their pebbled drive, as cars parked
and figures in black
stepped out, bearing food. At sundown

the girl's parents appeared
at the door. She leaned on him
as they stepped down
into grass. For years they'd go away

and I'd walk the dead girl's dog. Searching
all over their house
in thunderstorms. Lights
blinking on, speakers
thundering hymns. I'd find him
eventually, beneath a bed, in a closet,
shivering; eyes thick
with cataracts, tumors
beneath his scant,
white fur. Pulling him out, lifting him up

in my arms, leashing and dragging him out
into the rain.

Five-and-Dime, Scarsdale

In the five-and-dime
downtown, after school,
I tried on the sun
-glasses; then asked
the old man, How much
for these? A woman
in a fur coat asked me,
Where do you live?
I told her. I see,
she smiled at the man,
while I put the sun
-glasses back in their place.

The Abused Girl

She and I were
in the same class. A friend
said she liked me
but we barely
spoke. Was it because
she smoked
that I found her
so tempting? One morning
she was gone; they'd taken her
to inspect her
body for signs. I felt
such kinship then! as if
we'd be married
one day, as if
we already were. One morning
she came back.
We never learned
what had happened
to her father.
We shot baskets
side by side in
the gym, set apart
from the others
by choice. Desire
for her body
kept me close; but that
was as close
as I could bring myself
to her.

Another Mother

A mother watches another mother die.
Her son, the living one's, between them.
He's speaking with the dying, answering
her question: Will you be a poet
one day? He answers her that of course
he already is. She kisses him, or he drops
his cheek to be kissed. Her lips remind
him of a rubber tree he conjures somewhere
in the tropical sun. His mother waits and watches.

His friend, the dying woman's son, is gone
at school. Her husband the oncologist
sits sobbing in the sofa. She's dying
in their living room in June. A Catholic
whose family disowned her for marrying
this Jew. She was a nurse when she met him

and they had three sons. She would shout
but wouldn't mean it. She'd wear her robe
all day on weekends. Was she depressed?
Did she smoke in secret? She liked to read
her newspapers religiously, and purchase
their groceries in north Jersey. She's fifty
when she dies, maybe fifty-five. We say,

We'll let her rest. We'll visit again soon,
as we slip out and drive home in silence.

Father says, It's nature's way. Forking
another piece of meat into his mouth. He,
who had never tried to know her, will not
look up from his plate. While my mother
sits at the bottom of the table
watching me still, suddenly: found out.

Dogs

Chipper was depressed. All day long
he'd lie in the sun, and then shade
as crumbs fell down on his useless forepaws,
his long noble snout and dour
dun crown. As we children stepped on
his fanned tail. Sometimes we'd find him
standing on his hind legs, or squatting
on the tabletop: a gargoyle
devouring our dinner. Our father
would kick him to send him flying
with such hot licking yelps, howling
into the void of our dank basement.

Mikey's liquid eyes were always
infected, excrescent black nits
tangling his honeyed locks. He'd fight all
comers in the lane, demonically smiling
while overtoppling Chipper's
tall lean frame. Then humping him to prove
a point. Dozing beneath the bench,
his clubbed tail browbeating Chipper's
Galilean gaze. To curb him
we'd choke him, pulling and yanking
Mikey's neck until that black-lipped wet
mouth wept. One day I found they'd left

pools of blood on the tile. Shivering,
hunched over. Embarrassed. Retching
blood into their water bowls. Blood
matting their collapsing haunches.
They disappeared. We were told
it was a sickness that children
could not catch from dogs. But was it

poison? At dinner my father
cutting into his meat would ask,
Where did you get this? And how long
did you cook it for? And she'd smile
up the table at him: *You speak
as if I could poison my own
family.* Years later they purchased

a pug. Ginger, stampeding down stairs
and cracking into walls, stunned
but indomitable. She grew
to hate us all: bullet-like turds
left on the carpet on my mother's
side of the bed. And in return
Mother would feed Ginger chocolates
whenever she could. Then tell us,
*If she slips out and runs under
the wheels of our reversing car,
no one has to know.* And we'd laugh
at such mordant wit. Taking care

of a sister's friend once, who would not
do what I said, I took his arm
and squeezed. Until he cried and fled
up the stairs. I was ashamed, I felt
such tenderness for him then! But my fear
was greatest for myself. Ginger

survived. We found her a home
with a shut-in who desired
a dog that would do its business
indoors. As we pulled up she leapt
from our car; we found her reveling
in a garden of trash. My mother cradled
the dog to her breast like she'd never
done before, as we climbed the steep
brownstone steps together.

A Visit

Placed in the pee-stained easy
chair, cross-legged like a woman
with the cuff of his black
slacks revealing a stretch
of pallid shin, sagging
black socks. He downed his cup
of tap water. Petted
our guilty dogs. He was concerned
for our attendance. Where
is your husband? Counting
the children before him
he said, There is a son
missing? While the first
snowflakes fell. We will try
to be better, Father,
she promised. While the dogs
leapt and yelped, we said
goodbye, and shut the door
on him forever.

Four Signs

He left and came home
again. Both of his palms
bleeding. He blamed it on
black ice. His teeth

were rotting. The dentist
said, Son, you have the mouth
of a man already climbing
into the grave. Holding

the bow wrong, the vanes
sliced through. His hand
bloated like a drowned man, the gash
grinned. Recently I heard

he'd hit a car. The man
asked him, What the hell's
the matter with you? are you trying
to get yourself killed?

A Leaf

He was trembling
like one, Mother said
Father said
about my brother
in the hospital bed;
as if surprised
at what he'd almost
done. Giddy, too,
because he'd have to
try it again. So much
had changed! or would be
changing soon. Was he scared
he'd be punished,
this life or the next? Or

was it guilt that made him
tremble like a leaf
on a high branch
of the tall oak
outside the window
he'd opened to fit
his small body

through? Forget this was
in winter, forget
the oak had been
evergreen. He fell

like an act of truth
and beauty
spiraling down
to the melting

snow.

Wouldn't it seem
a miracle if
it had happened at all

this way?

Sister

What did you know then?

In the house below our mother tied up
her knot of blood.

He sobbed like blood leaves
a wound.

The body is the mystery,
I knew then.

How can you not know what occurred?

Playing with you
on the floor, cold
because the window
he'd jumped from
was still open.

I must have forgotten you.
Forgive me,

I was afraid to tell you
what I didn't know.

Meat on the Fire

To light the fire I'd bring the torch
up from the basement, where they kept
my brother's old pornography
in damp cardboard boxes. In springtime
this room would flood, the warped
linoleum grinding free from
the convoluted cement beneath.
Sliding the bolt across my head
blindly with some terror for
the spider in the web my hand
swept through; then out the door I'd climb
into summer living twilight

and strike the spark in the hissing
jet, bathe the coals in the propane's
cobalt tongue; till that stacked black pile
flamed, then glowed. I was happiest there, alone
beside the house, with the neighbors'
kids behind the fence, the setting sun
a glob in the branches; tilting
to inhale the untainted air
outside the rising tumult
of smoke. I burnt their meat
most every night; then went inside
to sit and eat my dinner with them.

The Firecracker

was just waiting there
for me, water
-logged and fractured
beside some matches
on the windowsill
that looked out on
our suddenly profuse
backyard; in this house
where nobody spoke
to a mother
who could never
shut up: I thumbed

open the slim
box, fumbled out
a wooden stick
and struck the head,
then passed the wet
wick through until
that mute fuse flared
to life – then popped
beneath my hand
as a glass thread
slipped in between
my ears. I ran

outside, my mother
behind, How
could you do this
to us? How could I

answer her when
I could not hear
a word she said

anymore?

Another Complaint

When they cut down the dogwood
we dismembered it with handsaws,
stacked and twined the limbs,
snapped the twigs and finer gray
tendrils in our raw, small hands,
crumpling buds in bunches
and bagging it in plastic
piled on the side of the road.

The stump remained an empty
plinth for weeks, as winter came
and evenings ate up our lawn.
My sister was done with school
(where my mother never went,
where my father never went),
where she'd majored in Fine Art
& Literature: now she took the train
to the city to work as the assistant
to an editor of *soft-core
pornography*, they liked to joke
about their eldest daughter,
when it was romance
literature for housewives
like our mother. I'd found
a poem she'd written that fall,
of a girl who kept slipping
down into the infernal
city sewers like she were nothing
more than a scrap of paper
filled with the beginnings
of a suicide note. In a few months
my father would kick her out
for crying too much. For Christmas

they exhumed her thesis
from the basement, a soldered bird
like a phoenix, certainly mythic
and almost funny for how
close it flew to art: serrated
feathers, shard-beaked, reptilian
talons and terrible wings
outstretched and flexed in gruesome,
frustrated flight. For some reason

no one could comprehend then,
our father and our mother
bolted that bird to that stump
facing the world, festooning
its iron wings with colored lights,
then left her there burning
well into a wet new year.

From Larchmont

On a bed of rock above the Sound
on Sundays in summer we'd sit
with each other and our black books,
yours for sketching, mine for writing
these poems like love for you. Streets away
past old folks' homes, *like the skeletons*
of whales, I mused, there was a church
I liked to pray in as a boy, gazing up
into the cruciform rafters dreaming, We
are each of us sailing in upturned boats
implausibly out of our protestant births
past grief, past silence, off this bed of rock
into this sea, this sound . . .

Gone Dog

Still young, I tried to go
out with her to dinner;
a movie, a hand job
in my mother's wagon
under the blinking
street lamp in an empty
parking lot. We had no friends;
we were romantically
marooned. Maybe it was the night
the police tapped on
the steamed glass, or the time
a rival team chased us
all the way to Yonkers
when they noticed the letter
on my breast. Or was it
the night nothing happened
at all? until we drove

down the dead end street
where my family
slept. Because I'd convinced her
to let me make love to her
finally. When a white dog leapt
into the road, not a dog
I'd seen before, no time
to brake before it glanced
under the passenger
side like a stone. She cried
like it was already
over. I stepped out

into the road
searching
the neighbors' yards
for what I deserved,

but that dog was gone,
just like I knew
it could be.

Patience

of Job, the young black woman said, in Lord
& Taylor. That's what you have, boy! Because I'd spent the day
folding ties and fanning them out
by color, like I'd been told to. I couldn't sell,
hadn't earned that right yet. I was too young
and this was my first job, standing all day in Men's Apparel
all week over holiday break. The old and new
came together in me: a martyr by birth
and a Jew by aspiration. An old woman asked me
one morning, thinking I was someone else, Are you
Christian? and unthinkingly I replied: I am.

Fixing the House

On a Saturday morning my father would wake me
with his impregnable stare, my name submerged
still in sleep, and stand in the doorway with no sympathy
for the rest of my adolescence. We'd be fixing the house
again, today. A new toilet seat maybe, or
that showerhead finally? Baths having been the only
choice in our youth, which was odd because a plumber
had been his true calling, having learned it from his father,
a failed plumber, someone once said. Or secondhand
linoleum tile, fresh caulking or sanding down
calloused walls, stripping wallpaper, ripping out carpets,
disempacting choked gutters and sweeping the floodwaters down
into the drain in our basement floor. I construed
this ruination of sleep as a love deferred, not decrepit,
and still we hated him for it. Because all day long

he'd be nasty. Sending you downstairs to his workbench
for tools you'd never heard of, much less seen, then berating you
for your ignorance; he'd command you, Lift this – no
not like that, like *this*! Then assign you the tasks
he'd never do himself, involving lead paint or
asbestos pipe-wrap, fashionable dangers he considered
overvalued; then he'd disappear for hours
only to return at dusk and say, What in God's name
have you done? – *all wrong, all wrong*, taking the tools
from out of your hands with the exasperated sigh
of a man who's asked so little of life and received

even less. – Oh! and then he'd curse all the way through it
as if to lubricate his disdain for the actions
he was called on to perform as the man of the house,
snaking a drain, say, of a clot of our mother's tangled
black hair. And what hair he still had would wilt over
the smeared glasses he peered through at this, yet another

unredeemable son – as if he'd never laid eyes
on such an idiot before! his favorite word
for the builder of our house, that ghost, whose asinine
decisions he was always unmaking in the walls
or ceiling, underneath our floorboards; for our neighbors
and teachers and that rare thing, a boss, and his own wife
too – *Idiots!* he'd sneer, and strangely I can't recall
once burning with shame at the word. If you were lucky

he'd send you to the hardware store. And if you lingered there
long enough, blaming traffic and lights, well then your day
was that much more done. The old men behind the counter
would ask after him; they'd worked here when he was a boy,
      running
errands for his old man. They'd never say anything
else about him. Which always made me wonder
if they harbored in their drowsy gray husks some kind of fondness
for the boy, at least a secret that might help explain

a man like this. After their store burned down
one summer night, he said the next morning as we bent
to plugged pipes: Jew lightning. Idiots. Now go get me my
      wrench . . .

The House in Scarsdale

'Because my mother got blamed for it. When
my brother, he was older, their only
son, firstborn. They sent him away, up north
to Calvary, I meant to say Calgary,
isn't that funny how the human mind
can work? unbeknownst to you. They did that
in those days, a home where they'd be able
to care for him, correctly. No one knows
what was wrong, today he would be diagnosed
I don't know what. I mean, who cares? he might
still be alive for all we know, somewhere
like Calvary. Yet they blamed her for it
so she began to drink. And she always
liked to drink but now she'd drink all day
and night, and once she almost killed me, or tried
to, tried to anyway. Because she was
trying to get out of our house to go
ask our neighbors for some vodka like some
people borrow flour, and she was wearing
only a bra and panties beneath
her mink stole. I stood between her and the door
while she screamed and beat me with her fists
and clawed my eyes out or tried to, tried to
anyway, and I laid my small body down
in front of the door so she could never
leave. And eventually she fell asleep
on the sofa. So that when my father came home
and found me scratched and bleeding, and my mother
passed out naked in the living room – well,
everyone knew my father could finally
divorce her. And keep us all together,
all his girls. – But why do we never blame the girls
or boys? when things go wrong at home. Help me

out on this one, Dan. Because my brother
tried to burn our house down, did you know that?
our mansion, we've driven past it, you've seen
its crimson brick face through trembling oak leaves,
its twin marble lions flanking a white
crushed seashell drive. I wonder who lives there
now? That house was haunted! I mean, it was
a tomb! Thirty rooms on seven acres
with the most memorable view of the Sound
beyond. The highest in the county. Hill,
I've heard said, the highest hill. With ceilings
that were too tall and so many rooms full
of nothing. Cursed. Is the word. I would wander
from room to room. We had maids, and Arthur
our black butler from New Orleans who was
gay, which was all right then, so long as no one
said a word. And that dilapidated
greenhouse we used to hide in when we played,
and a backyard that sank into
unfathomable woods. Auld Ridge, it was called
by the original millionaire-builder,
but as a child I called it Old Ditch, where
I lived until I married your father,
a plumber. I never finished college.
Which was all right because I wanted that
then. Poverty, then. Which is why we had to
elope, which is why we have so little
money now. Or not much anyway.
Because eventually my father took pity
on us all, and bought us this house in Scarsdale
so that our children at least would not suffer.'

Dorset

The unconstrained stars over Dorset
as if constellations had been cut
free of their bonds. Above mountaintops
like an ocean arrested. Twisting
runt trees in the orchard, crab apples
rotting in the dew-gleamed grass. How crass

they'd become! just because they'd bought their mansions
from nothing. Study business, he'd said
with a drink in the claw
of his arthritic hand. His gardener infected
with AIDS wheeling over their pastures
on their riding lawnmower. We were laughing
at the absurdity of their paying
such a man. While secretly I dreamed

I'd become a nature poet
someday, somehow. Close to the school
they paid for up north. Me, the unannounced
king. Only a year till he died, only a decade more
till they turned their backs on me. – But those trees!

like hands upstretched. Death's mountaintops
encroaching. I am still in love with wealth,
it would seem.

An Eye

My father recalled hummingbirds
in the bare trees outside a restaurant
in Vermont. Where I remembered a creek
he described gentle cataracts weaving
through woods at dusk. Neither of us could recall
the season, or the occasion. When the rich man

handed me the keys to his luxury car
to drive the family to dinner, his glass eye
leering at the thistle, as if searching
for the eyeball he'd lost in a wreck
last winter, driving his previous luxury car
through a blizzard and the South Bronx to work
on Broadway. He looked down on their marriage, now
three decades old, because his daughter
had gotten pregnant. Or that's what I don't know

yet. At dinner the rich man's younger, second wife
studied my face sidelong. Concerning a career
in the arts, she advised, Oh
he'll be all right. Provided
you can keep an eye on him.

On Leaving

All summer waiting
for the end to come
without knowing
where I'd go. I'd promised
to leave; yet leaving
felt like suicide. While staying
home would be a kind
of death, too. So I walked

in the mornings down
to the bridge to watch
the white water fall
and slide under my feet
into the sucking
eddies of mud
and sticks and songs
of the unseen birds.

Castle White Apartments

The transistor radio
beneath the pillow. With the faux
Southern drawl. These ghostly guests.
That tortured pile of messed
white sheets and burning light motes
roiling in a ray. The throat
of the dim hallway leading

outside, where the lilies
hummed, encased in their glassy,
earthen veins. And the feathering
ferns beneath keening limbs
coiling into their entwined
likenesses. Scales of ivy
fluttering in the uni's
emerald courtyard, where the young
men and women played. The lungs

of the missing student were
full of river. My mother
was waiting for me to fail
and come home. The blind hall

-way back to those twisted white
sheets. The radio as night
returned. This consoling novel
I'd purchased of magical

realism.

Greenwich / Isle of Dogs

Down beneath river past strangers to rise
and sit in the maritime pews with all
midnight mass aglow below and hearing
nothing of the remonstrating sermon
but in love with my self and this young stray's life.

Pay Phone

You were right I do remember
fondly calling in a panic
from the pay phone
in the lobby of a hotel,
whilst inside the bar the Irish
were just getting going; along
the Western Road; and here I was
crying on maybe the sixth day
and confessing I'd failed
to escape you. You sounded
unsurprised. Or had it been

a phone booth in Thomastown? after
a day spent waiting on the bench
beside the graveyard for my girl
to come from *Amerikay*, nothing
to do here, simply admiring
some sparrows alighting, who spoke,
it seemed to me then, of my life
to come, as they argued for roof
-top sun; auguring, *Whatever*
will come is meant to be, like the leaves
enchanted in an autumnal
roll along the slate-plated roof
of that granary silo-cum
-Fine Arts School. This was the time when
you told me, as if with wonder
and fear, You've picked up a touch
of the brogue. And the violet light
outside that closed box shook and sang.

I can't remember if it was the time
I was hopeful, or the time I cried,
when you said, One day you will remember
when you were brave and suffered,
and you will find yourself longing
to be this way again.

The Limerick Station

That first morning the girls
wore skirts and blouses,
hustling for their buses
with wet hair swinging. While I searched
in circles, embarrassed
to ask. Inside the station

the patois of young men
like a clamor
of silverware spilled out
across the marble floor. All knives
and forks and spoons; and nothing
to eat yet. I collapsed
on my bag of books and condoms
as the wide-vaulted chamber
zoomed with birds. At a party

with I-don't-know-who. Lights
in the hearth revolving
across a cave-painted
living room wall. They sat
a crazy old woman
beside me. Who's this
boy? she asked, *with the face
like a judge* . . . sweeping the broom
of her hand down the stone
of her face, as my family
across the ocean
laughed with them.

The Castle

The driver's never even been
to Dublin. Raining like a fever
dream, while the radio plays
country. Will you ever learn
the names of all these new trees? Breaks
in the hedgerows and the trash-strewn
gates provide a racing glimpse
of gypsies' shirts on lines, strung
between swayback horses
and air. When you arrive
barking phantoms are waving
the cattails. The taxi's spitting
gravel. A motherly Canadian asks, *Who*

sent you now? Leading you down
her hallway hung with time-dimmed
tapestries. Chained mail and stained
-glass saints. Cardboard donation box
beside the phone. The receiver's
off the hook. Would you care to spend
the weekend? You're a patient
young man, I can see. I often speak
with the spirit of my husband,
and if you're lucky he'll speak
to you, too. Spanish newlyweds
descend to the table, kiss and coo
beneath a coat of arms. She'll give you

a room if you'll help her
tidy up her husband's library
of erotic literature
and art. Her sick son haunts
the bottom step watching

you with envy. Are you sure
you haven't been here before,
my love? And must you really
leave so soon?

First Pages of a New Journal

I

Days before Christmas, 23
-12-96, ten in the morning, Saint
Martin-in-the-Fields: What's this
like? to do nothing and say nothing
of any lasting value: I haven't written
a word in my life! What I need now
is an *asylum ignorantiae*, or something
quiet-by-the-sea. Bought a book
of Jung's work on dreams (because
you never know when something like that
might come in handy) last night
in Camden Town with N, and another
letter N-person I flirt with
because she's like that, too: I am
despairing prematurely. This coffee
shop in the crypt seems an outright
sacrilege, for instance my chair
stabbing the soft flat face of someone's
In Memoriam slab . . . Like Westminster
Abbey only vulgarer – *Orare
ancestors!* meaning 'pray for me'
in Latin, and I haven't because all
my life is falling from me
now. Nothing rises anymore. (Read

the Norse myths; go to the Nat'l
Gal., look at old paintings

there.)

2

Rembrandt: *Mene mene tekel upharsin*:
You have been measured and found
lonely. Or: you are a girl

stepping into her bath, gently lifting
up her skirts ... Words on a painting

here.

3

Back in the church above to pin
my prayer in the corkboard; to sit
in a stall and listen to the chamber
quartet mourning; to discover
words carved in the handrail,
Fuck God
         – when two men approach
with balls of keys ajangling
into the adjoining stall to unearth
a drunkard I hadn't yet noticed
there, sleeping away the day
on his face. *Would you care*

for some air, sir? And I wonder
if I should go now, too ...? *We don't mind*
the visiting, it's the lying down
we can't be having ...

'Where You From?'

In Cork City I tried to make myself
anew, or whom I wished I'd always been. When
the first Irish asked me, 'Where you from?'
I answered, 'The Bronx.' Because it made me seem

less this child of wealth, whom I did not believe
I was anyway; though I'd grown up
amongst them, had masqueraded as one
of them, could act the part too – I'd come here
in many ways thanks to them: it felt good
to lie. Until the performance was over

in the pub-theatre up the alley
from the churning Lee and its galleries
of bloody-tongued drunks, where all that fall
volunteers with their searchlights swept the slime
-slick walls, as the river trough at low tide
coughed up yet another market trolley
and other, less familiar debris,
for the body of a lost boy:

                              a friend
brought a girl from America. He saw me
pressing towards the bar and called my name
above the roaring throng – 'She's from the Bronx
like you!' I acted as if I could not hear

a word he said; then, as if I'd forgotten something
overwhelming, fled down the stairs and paced
the black river home to wherever
I was staying.

Fountainstown

Thomas, do I remember that day well?

Trespassing through an orchard
down to someone else's shore
with your brother and his girl,
who carried their surprising child
in her belly like a stone
inside one of those rude plums
that seemed to spin as we strolled
beneath them. Easter almost,
we debated the Church's
most recent abuses. Your girl
was there: matronly Anne,
forgive me, was older
than you, the scholarly fool
as all young brothers ought to be
abused and reminded just whom
they'd been till that day – all for this stranger,
and Anne who loved you more
for your shame. I wanted to be
a brother to you all, and not
some shy, proud interloper
whose secret he carried
inside him like a seed
that could never see water.

In the cove the sunlight
became wintry again. Shedding
your clothes on the grinding strand,
you called for me to join your
young faces rising in the swell.

The Bells

Palm Sunday on the floor
of someone else's flat
in the shadow of the Church
of Ireland spire, sleeping
before the blowing grate
on warped floorboards. The girl
I loved was coming and
together we'd go home
to marry. The ringing bells
awoke me to the blood
sausage and the murmuring
of the faithful sweeping
their palms along the road
to Easter.

Clear Island

Traipsing home drunk
around a bend
almost lunar
with stars and the moon
dilating, dreaming
of the envious
sidhe susurrating
the sea grass, hill weeds;
half-awaiting

the sodden steps
of a traveler, a nature
spirit twinkling
death from an eye
like a furious
wink. This island

romance a balm. Home

to my sleeping
lover dreaming
a bird was flying
right into her

open

mouth!

Via Waterford

The truth is I wanted to be
caught, as I climbed up out of
that borrowed town, to the train depot
in the pink-green, tabular field
of goats, who crunched on the bias
and watched me with their onyx, as if Orphic
eyes. One brother had given me
a camera for my trip. A sister
whispered in the folds of her letter: You
are a stranger to us, finally. Pilgrims
conversing in the twilit meadow
and gravel, waiting for the train
to arrive in a spark of light
in the kindling trees. Where was I
going? Home to the narrow room
with narrow bed and narrow window
via Waterford.

Black Pool

This was in a bar in the northside in the day,
Blackpool, I think it's called. I don't know why
I was there, who with. I remember
what might have been called an epiphany though
it happened like a seed grows underground: seeing
a woman through shop glass wheeled out
into the street in a hospital gown, in a bed
amidst the trash and traffic, like a tree limb
at the end of a flooding sweeping stream she
was whirled around to the gaping mouth
of the idling ambulance. A plastic bag
like a child's idea of the soul wafting
over her head. Was she ashamed of herself? She was
already dead in the eyes. I thought, Who will be waiting
there for me? I decided: This lesson is to stick
to your own blood, no matter what. So I went home
and swallowed ten more years.

The Wooden Box

I dreamed I owned a wooden box
and cleaned it with a rag and knife;
off with shavings came these clots
of dirt, and where not burnished
holes appeared. A voice whispered,

Your box is buried in the ground.

My Mother

Water in the bowl after
the flowers have been lifted out.

Danvers Wedding

So it's winter again. The snow
near Boston fell early. The wedding
party was both dismayed and impressed. The guests
drove fearful along the white-blind road
to Danvers . . . Old part of the country,
the grim driver said, one of a hundred
middle-aged and some very old
men at the wheel, spine-curved and brows
clenched, as their flighty wives delivered
directions to the yachting club in Danvers . . .
We were sad and angry to be so.
Who wants to be reminded what's lost,
or will be soon? No one cries
for happiness, really . . . The bride and groom
clung to each other
inside the stone church.

Providence

I

Just a small room
in a house full of books,
with a motley collection
of pens and papers. Butcher's
brown for wrapping
with twine. Scissors and tape
and loose stamps from before
you were born. These poets
used to send their poetry
into the world. The snow
lines the limbs and trash
cans in the backyard.

2

Like any Edward Hopper
painting: together, alone
in the mostly forgotten square
not far from the school
while sleet skims the fogged
windowpane. Who could have known
this night would be waiting
here for you? Eating the light
off a scratched plastic plate.

The Consolation of Poetry

Otherwise, dear brother,
I'd be where you are now,
where they've taken away
your belt and shoelaces; where
all you can do is call
home for help.

Bread Loaf 1994

How dark it is in
the old house atop
the hill, where the no-name
middle-aged men remained
sequestered with two
aspirant poets. They'd asked us
to bring the girls;
they would scare up
the faggots, they laughed
to each other: meaning
the sticks for the fire
in the yard beside
the house. But no fire
got lit, they sat on
our louche porch instead,
drinking and reading
poems they'd written on God
knows what, impotence,
divorce, death, youth,
ambition and failure . . . the rote
invocations of
everybody's suffering
rising in the gloam.
Then they'd laugh again,
below my bed where
I lay believing I'd be greater
than them all. When my family

left, summer over, they wouldn't
step inside. They raised
their heads to the windows
instead. Reflected
leaves in warped glass. This

would be the house where
I will remain for
the rest of my life, these old men
my true fathers. Shuddering
down the shifting road
they fled. My roommate

had been out with a girl
in his mother's car
in the woods. He sat
in bed in the spill
of the moon, proud
and embarrassed of this
love bite on his neck,
what with his sister's
wedding in the morning:
Can you tell? I lied,
No. He said, You should've
come with! There was someone
there for everyone. Have you ever
seen a black girl nude? I said,
Not yet. Her skin was like
the night, this young poet
told me: the truth is it never
seems to end.

I Fear the Grief that Comes with Age

I had a teacher who told me
I had what it took to become
a writer like him, maybe
better. Or so I liked to think.
He'd read what I'd write only
cursorily; it was enough
to acknowledge my greatness
with vagueness. Sporting a dead man's
tweed to class, reading at my teacher's
right elbow. Gazing through the window
on a womb of limestone, the snow
-blessed branches a seeming paean
to loneliness. Shivering in his car

with filthy toys and scraps of food
underfoot. His beard was gray
and his wife a painter. She told me
once in passing, in the underground
office of Religion where she answered
the phones, how proud my teacher was
of me. I blushed, still young. She died
several summers ago, still young.

I came to class early
and one of the other children had written
my name on the board,
as if I would teach them
that day – as if I could ever
teach anyone anything!

The Amphitheatre

Up from an evening's sleep
in the communal room
full of friends, the window
a slate of churning
snow. When the storm was through
we went outside into

a flood of moonlit drifts,
feet numbing, lips rent, breath
adhering into ice
in our new beards. By way

of the Catholic graveyard,
profaning only
when our boots found the crowns
of buried tombstones. Growing
silent without knowing
why. Plowing
wide lanes through fine sere snow
between rows of firs
that arched with still more snow
like grief. Into the well

of the amphitheatre,
in the yard of some
rich man's house. To wait
speaking softly about
Nature, Art, that bright dome
of abyss above. One night

a light blinked on inside
the rich man's house. We peered in at him
peering out at us. Before
he turned out the light.

Engagement

Flew all night to land at dawn
the morning we chose the design.
All day a fisherman made
the gold ring. Calling home that night
from a roadside booth beneath
a blown bulb. It was afternoon
where they were. Astonished
by our good fortune. Next morning standing
in the hotel room watching
the window wash with rain, I thought
I should live here, why couldn't we
live here? In the library, empty,

like the church next door. Someone
said someone I'd known had died
at home. Running in the mist
along the inlets of the bay
seeing no one, breathing coal.
That night in our bright bed
beside your bright body, your face
brightening my face. I thought maybe
I'd been wrong to fear so much
for so long. Then driving before dawn

along murderous cliffs, swerving
to avoid the sleeping
sheep like children in the road. Terrified
of the high horns of the red stag
whose reflective eyes seemed
to prophesy something worse
was coming, surely. Climbing the plains

with the sun, scornful of the warming
blue, thinking, Why hadn't I lived
here instead? Why couldn't I stay?

The Last Time

When the dog in the grass threw up
on my shoes, the family laughed again. When
you saw my head uncovered. When
we stood on chairs in the sun
praising him. You're jealous, I said.
You're right, I've always been jealous
of my son. Absconding from the service
in your boyish blue blazer. Whistling
across the quadrangle for shade,
you asked the bride, Aren't you ashamed
of him? and at home told me: You look
like someone about to slit
his own throat. While another son
measured the rope. Our mother clinging
to your side like someone who could
love you now. Her lunatic smiling in spite
of herself. Let's go for a walk then,
you and I. Why? There are things
you do not know. Tell me. There are things
you do not know. While my brothers
and sisters slept through the night, I walked
out for the last time. In the morning
along the highway I ate
nothing but your red meat.

The Wrong Son

But could it be? My first memory

I've been left alone to wait
at the bottom of the stairs. Gauze curtains soaking
up afternoon sun. My mother whispering
to the ghost over my head. Who hands me

the Bible? as I play at his feet. Shamanic
beard and wild hair, running away
before we wake up. One night he calls

when nobody's home, and he speaks
to my suicidal brother. Drunk,
my brother later says. Where he was
my brother can't say. What they talked of
nobody knows. But did my uncle know

when he'd hung up the phone that he'd almost confessed
to the wrong son?

Gramercy

That play we went to see near Gramercy
Park at the end of the last century
in the afternoon, one of those summery
days in fall, one of those sad auld tales
written by the Irish I left you for. After
the morning you rode the subway
for the first time since you were a girl,
you told me, swerving upright with your bag
in your hands beside me as the empty
car shifted and shrieked and the lights stammered
out. Mother and son in the dark house watching
the age-old drama conclude. Then strolling
downtown after, with bankers descending

into the melee of the streets. Struggling
to hail you a taxi. You said: One day
you will live here. And how will I ever know
if you envied or condemned me
before vanishing into that everyday scene?

Truro

This is not to say we were not brought to the beach
once a year, walking out on the burning

sands as one family away
from those families we despised

for their boom boxes, their wheeling kites, their gratuitous
beer bellies. He'd march us out farther

along the shoreline, where once in our exodus
with our lives on our backs, it would seem, he said to me

as if I were a notion, or a fencepost: Your brother
will never marry. This was adolescence; I was concealing

erections in the towel beneath my belly
against the curving sand, and once

a girl not far away dozed
flat on her back, the vee of her wet suit askew

and my father winked and said, Now there's
an education for you . . . Launching

ourselves into the waves
at low tide, waist- and then shoulder-high, then nothing

beneath our pedaling feet
with our mother behind us in the shallows smiling,

for once, our youngest brother on a rope buffeted
in his inflatable craft, in terror as the waves

washed over him and we brothers
and sisters rode the chaos in, wrecked

ourselves often, socked and spun and
up we'd come in joy with sand

in mouths and ears and crevices
– all of us children, except the one

who'd stayed home, who would never marry. I preferred
to face out towards the sea: the boundless sea

wasn't death yet. Our father never swam, he stood
rotund and pale atop a low dune. When you arrived

in the morning, the lovely youths
checked the sticker on your wagon; when you left

at end of day, the step from sand to pavement
was enough to break your hearts.

The Music House

The last room in the music house was mine
for a year, shared with the half-deaf teacher
of Faulkner and Joyce, whom I rarely saw,
coming as I did late at night when the school
was a sepulcher of sound, and the road
a treacherous skin of ice. I'd walk here
to sit in the human-like hiss of the steam
-heat, the scent of all those moldering scores
and the stowaway ghost of pine. The dregs
of coffee drunk mid-afternoon. To wait
for the first time. Until a student came
whose footsteps were like a twin to mine:
listening through the wall as he played
over and over the same old song.

CB *editions*

Founded in 2007, CB editions publishes chiefly
short fiction (including work by Will Eaves, Gabriel
Josipovici, David Markson and Todd McEwen)
and poetry (Beverley Bie Brahic, Nancy Gaffield,
Stephen Knight, J. O. Morgan, D. Nurkse). Writers
published in translation include Apollinaire,
Andrzej Bursa, Joaquín Giannuzzi, Gert Hofmann,
Agota Kristof and Francis Ponge.

Books can be ordered from www.cbeditions.com.